L'Amarcable

A Nature to Nurture

By
Michael Irving

Photographs by
Michael Irving
and Chris L'Amarca

For Chris

Thank you for believing in nature
and believing in me.

For Grace

Guess what? I love you!

"The goal of life is to make your heartbeat match the beat of the universe, to match your nature with Nature."

—Joseph Campbell

Foreword:
Fostered by Nature

Nature is not about standing out nor reaching the top. It is about thriving and, if need be, surviving—simply to carry on. Thus, I may not be disciplined or ambitious enough to align myself within nature. Though, I hope, at the very least, to understand nature and relate to it in a way that I can support its care and promote a love for it among others. It is a conglomerate of life I hope we will all have faith in it being there everyone tomorrow.

We will all be orphans at some point in our lives. Whether by death, separation, or self-protective isolation, we will, no matter how hard we try to resist it, realize the experience of being alone.

We may find ourselves alone, isolated from humanity, at some points in our lives. Though, if we appreciate her, honor her, and protect her—yes,

"The goal of life is to make your heartbeat match the beat of the universe, to match your nature with Nature."

—Joseph Campbell

Foreword:
Fostered by Nature

Nature is not about standing out nor reaching the top. It is about thriving and, if need be, surviving—simply to carry on. Thus, I may not be disciplined or ambitious enough to align myself within nature. Though, I hope, at the very least, to understand nature and relate to it in a way that I can support its care and promote a love for it among others. It is a conglomerate of life I hope we will all have faith in it being there everyone tomorrow.

We will all be orphans at some point in our lives. Whether by death, separation, or self-protective isolation, we will, no matter how hard we try to resist it, realize the experience of being alone.

We may find ourselves alone, isolated from humanity, at some points in our lives. Though, if we appreciate her, honor her, and protect her—yes,

Mother Earth and Mother Nature—we will never be without the company of either.. Let us not estrange ourselves from our family of nature. For, in doing so, we are, even if it seems we are not in how slowly we do it, abandoning life itself.

On March 31, 2023 I was challenged to overcome my despair-stricken isolation and reunite with nature. I was challenged by a dear friend from far away that I have never met face-to-face. Up until then, I felt hopeless from an accumulation of losses that seemed far greater than any gains. I was giving up on everything that was a part of my life—one by one I was prematurely surrendering to my own mortality. Yes, while our mortality is inevitable, one could say that I was headed for my own sooner rather than later. But, in truly witnessing one who will pass far sooner than me, I knew I must stop asking for forgiveness for the neglect of myself and my surroundings. I knew that I must forgive myself for not thinking that I am worthy of being present with myself and nature and caring for the both. I knew that I must honor this dear friend as best as I could for she has honored me with her time that is much less abundant than my own.

This is my heartfelt tribute to Chris L'Amarca through what she loves so much—what she loves like her own family, for it is a family as well to her. Yes, that is her nature family.

This is the nature I discovered and, in discovering it, I discovered more about Chris and more about myself.

I do not just celebrate Chris through this newfound appreciation of nature. I also celebrate my daughter who has inspired me to breathe and simply enjoy those joyfully dusty, dirty, and muddy moments with nature. This mud's for you!

The 1st Spot in Nature
Ewing Trace

State of Mind Line Road

"Awareness is without choice, without demand, without anxiety; in that state of mind, there is perception."

—Bruce Lee

The second city of my life has always been Kansas City. Though I have stayed in many homes in this metropolitan area—from those of my Aunts to my Grandparents to my Sister and to my Mother and Stepfather—each residence has had its place in my heart as a home to me.

Kansas City was formed, in great part, from the junction of the Kansas and Missouri Rivers as a prime commercial location. Kansas and Missouri thus share the city of Kansas City. The dividing line between these states, though not a border in the sense that borders have sadly been stigmatized related to ethnicity and nationality, that runs through Kansas City is State Line Road. Though, this dividing line blends the differences of each state, whatever they may be, through culture and shared pride for a city that both states have in common. No, it is not Kansas City, Missouri the joyfully raucous nor Kansas City, Kansas the blissfully calm. It is Kansas City, Kansas and Missouri like two dedicated chambers in the heart of our lives.

On a walk today though the city in which I live, Des Moines, Iowa, I found myself on a road that seemed divided by nature's fight for relevance and the urban dweller's fight for, sometimes unchecked, freedom. The cars were traveling far above the posted speed limit—one who actually obeys the posted speed makes himself or herself out to be the outcast—on the road that seemed no more than ten feet from the sidewalk where I was walking. I feared a loss of

control at any moment by any of the drivers where a

car would careen over the curb destroying anything,

including me, in its path. But, I still could hear, like the

spirit of the underdog, the songs of the birds that had an

honored stake in nature just twenty to thirty feet from

the road.

What was the driving force that compelled me to leave the house? What was the greater prize than staying inside? Nature and a champion of it, my good friend Chris! Roads are built, changed, or repaired when enough people raise their voices as to

what needs to be done with such a road in regards to

their personal concerns. Scare tactics such as what

neglecting this road would do to the local economy might be an example of such spoken words. Though, who speaks up for nature? Who speaks up for the trees, the birds, and the ever so vital bees? Not enough of humanity it sadly seems.

If others could only have heard the voice in my head today, a voice that was not my own but still more trusted than the archetypal angel on one's shoulder. It was the voice of my friend capturing and preserving my appreciation for the snippets of authentic nature that seemed to fight for their existence through the voice of their beauty and value to our continued humanity. It is nature in the fields of emerging green grass that waved in exaltation like a self-choreographed stadium of fans at a baseball game. Trees hunched the sidewalk in their breezy psithurism as if they were saying, "I, unlike a building, grow and give you the air you breathe."

May we never be too busy to smile. May we never be too busy to be in awe of this nature that gives us the air we need—yes, this nature we need. We just cannot be too busy to breathe.

"I see them bloom for me and you."

-Louis Armstrong

Inner Voices of Nature and Friends

"Nature... is nothing but the inner voice of self-interest"

—Charles Baudelaire

Is it possible to exercise a memory? That is, might thinking about, talking about, or writing about a memory make it stronger? Scientifically speaking, I would think so.

Emotionally speaking, they say that talking about something gets it out of our heads. Though, I would think and will, therefore, trust that applying our senses to memories makes them stronger.

I believe that nature is a spiritual gym that can strengthen our memories. It is a place where a person like me, a trained introvert, can evolve into a spiritual extrovert. Though, it may take some motivation to get there—an inner mentor if you will.

Yes, what does that unique voice inside of us say that leads us to what is best for us? Is it a voice of no one in particular or the voice of someone we know that we can imagine saying what is best for us through compassion and wisdom? And, does that inner voice even need to say anything at all? For, we communicate to be heard through more than just words, don't we?

My inner voice on this day is the calm enunciations of acknowledgment and reassurance in the voice of my friend Chris. My inner voice is also the sound of bird songs and the breeze telling me that it is okay to come outside to nature—that there is life out here.

On the mornings that I feel as though I can't move, I will take the memories of nature and the conversations with my friend as my call to move me.

Like a Four-Legged Friend at the Door

"A friend may be nature's most magnificent creation." - Ralph Waldo Emerson

It has been more than twenty years ago since I was last here. I know they were not waiting for me, the trees and all of their compatriots of nature that is, but they are still here like I remember. Still here with a purr of the wind through the branches and the ripples of the waters.

They are still here like your cat at the door when you arrive home from work. Still here like a good friend that has looked after your hometown in all the years you have been gone.

With this reunion you have so much to talk about it seems. You take all the pictures you can to share with your friend that has stepped in like a family member through the bewilderment of how life goes on without the family of old. Though, in this nature where you remember those "good old days," nature welcomes you unconditionally. And, rain or shine in your heart, a good friend does the same.

A good friend greets you like a refreshing wind when you walk out the door that knocks you on your behind in the joyful collision. A good friend is like your four-legged friend at the door when you get home from work—unconditionally present.

Nature is a good friend. Chris is a good friend. Therefore, Chris is a friend to nature and nature is a friend to Chris.

Life Lessons Through Mother Nature's Curriculum

"Experience is the mother of wisdom."
—British Proverb

Another rumble, but it is not thunder. Another flash, but it is not lightning. Terrors to the ego seemingly persist through broad daylight or the pitch black of midnight. They must have chosen a subwoofer cranial spasm over the serenity of nature. Me? I'll take curtain number two's palpable midnight crisp air and its soft green grasses spotted with dew.

Twigs are nature's drumsticks. A locust seed pod or two in each hand make nice maracas. And below your feet or below your sitting bum is the earth that makes for a pretty good drum. Though, be gentle with them. Allow them to settle so they can grow again.

A great teacher does not give you the answers you need. A great teacher inspires your curiosity and drive to find the answers you need. And, along the way, you learn not just the answer to the questions you have. You also are inspired with greater curiosity to learn more.

I have a teacher in the school system of nature. Her name is Chris. She has inspired me to wonder how the trees, the sky, the earth, and the animals can so fluidly co-exist while we the people seem to make our co-existence more complicated than it needs to be.

May We Learn to Nurture from How It Nurtures Us

"Learn how to see. Realize that everything connects to everything else."

—Leonardo da Vinci

They don't ask for the rain, but they silently hope it will come. They have faith that, in the next day, they will see and feel the sun.   While we may make demands for more than we need, which is really what we want, they instinctively know what they need and how they must go about finding it.

Once we believed in extending an olive branch to make friends or amends in our connections. Now, we, well some, often drain all we can from one or something then we move on. In their flocks, their schools, or their groves they seek and they share. The weaker are made stronger by the community. Even in what they leave behind, though unfavorable to our liking I'm sure, you have to admit that it is one way of giving back to the earth. I hope humanity can apply the same principle.

May we nurture those that nurture nature and the earth. May we wonder with concern when we step out the door and don't hear the sound of a bird's song, feel the grass as cool and soft between our toes, or pass through the aromatic force field of pansies, daisies, and pine that greets us and preserves our hope for nature. May we wonder with the concern of where has it gone and what can we do to bring it back?

Nature, absent of the interference of humanity, is universally beautiful. Though, a wise humanity can uphold or restore any part of nature's beauty that has been lost. There are advocate for nature among us like the angels that I believe are among us too. If an advocate or an angel does not come to mind, empower yourself to be one. If you need the inspiration to become one, think of Chris, for she already believes in you!

An Outdoors Homecoming

"Hiking is not escapism; it's realism. The people who choose to spend time outdoors are not running away from anything; we are returning to where we belong."

— Jennifer Pharr Davis

Some, possibly many, of those that love nature run from a world where others have pretended that what was never real was real to them for so long that they and many others have come to accept the cruel and implausible as acceptable and true. Suffering is either sadly denied or horrifically entertaining. Compassion sadly threatens the exposure of one's insecurity. And life is no longer lived in the community of humanity and nature.

My home has become an escape from what feels like an insecure humanity where it seems that many, but of course not all, do not wish to take the time to listen, to evaluate, or to feel an emotion. Therefore, I have realized that I nature as a nutrient that my soul lacks.

Home is not always a building, but it must always be place where we feel that we belong. It provides us with an appreciation for life and a cause to live for. It raises us with self-respect and a respect for life outside of our own.

Though my friend lives thousands of miles away and we have never met face to face, we welcome each other home each day to the home we share in nature. I'll see you in the home of nature soon my friend.

Nature With and Within

"Never, no never, did nature say one thing and wisdom another."

—Edward Burke

Our earthly carousel reminds us to hold hope for tomorrow while making the best of today. Keep your presence inside this ride at all times, or for as long as you can. For, to focus your regret on yesterday or your fears upon tomorrow, you may lose what your mind is trying to process, your heart is trying to feel, and your soul is trying to store.

Nature is where I hope to be found when what has commonly been seen and experienced of me is gone. But, I hope that will be the best of me without the worst of me getting in the way. It is my great hope that I will realize a soul's loving fortune in being a part of what has inspired peace and appreciation in my life—always in the heart of my daughter and always a part of the spirit of nature.

Who I am as well as who I could become will never be more than a "Who?" without the inspiration of a dear friend that parted the limbs and the leaves for my shadow to be seen among the shadows in nature. For, my walk with nature has been like trying on clothes as a child and tiptoeing out of the dressing room so as not to draw the snicker or the ire of another. Though, upon the smiles and my own smile at myself in the mirror, I believe that I was meant to wear the peace and joy of what nature has fashioned for me—for everybody!

Yes, like a fashion consultant, though really a consultant to the soul, I can just hear my dear friend say, "Nature looks beautiful on you and you look beautiful in nature."

She knows because she and nature do the same for one another. Nature would almost be without the light that brings it to life so beautifully without the company of Chris. And Chris would not have the same smile that spreads the horizon of the earth nor the same shine in her eyes that any pair of sunglasses could not possibly hide without the light, the breeze, the skies, and the seas of nature.

In Nature's Backyard

"Small steps taken by many people in their backyards add up."

-Nancy Knowlton

Whether by the borders or concealments of fences or even our own homes, our backyards are places often reserved for our privacy. Though, what might we miss when we are cut off from the world from morning to night? Who are we missing that needs us and that reminds us of our value in being the human part of nature? And, what do we need from others that we are afraid to ask for?

We may see nature as that which is in our backyard. Nature may see us and where we live as that which is in its backyard. Yes, the facade of our yards and homes may be made to be envied. Though, often our backyard exists as it does so that it can be shared. Let us share in the love of a park, lake, stream, or tree. Let us share in the company of nature for it cannot be our nature to do with as we please. Let us get out to be in nature with every breath we have to care for nature so that we are allowed another day to breathe.

Yes, I live in nature's backyard.

While I am encouraged by my friend to be a part of nature, by her practice I am reminded that nature is not just a part of me but something greater than myself to which I have a responsibility.

Another? Yes, Another Reason to Smile

"When the root is deep, there is no need to fear the wind."

—African Proverb

What is the loss of one tree when there are over three trillion trees on earth? Sure, there are enough trees for 430 billion birds on earth to perch on, one billion dogs to sniff and mark, and 184 billion rolls of toilet paper to be used each year. Yes, these don't account for all of the trees in the world, so the loss of another tree is not something many of us lose sleep over at night.

Though, I think of the people who can't leave their homes or cannot look out their windows to see a tree—if they have a window that is. I remember the last view my father had was through his hospital window. Standing directly outside of his window was a young tree in full bloom. Birds from Robins to Cardinals to I swear what must have been the state bird themselves, Goldfinches, frolicked through the branches and leaves and lounged on the limbs.

That tree gave the birds a jovial jungle gym and home. The birds and the tree itself gave my father, and I swear to this belief to this very day, an inspired dream for his next life. For, when he turned his head to look out the window, I could see the crook of his weak, though still prominent, smile.

Deeper roots make for stronger trees. Friendships that are deep in shared memories, feelings, and mutual support make for stronger, though still tender, hearts. Through the support of my dear friend Chris, I have been able to withstand the windstorms of grief through my roots of gratitude, humor, contemplation, and compassion.

Another tree is another reason for me to be in nature and not in isolation. Another tree is another topic for conversation between friends. Another tree is another reason to smile. And the smile of my friend is another reason for me to keep going.

Nurtured by Nature at Night

"And if you don't believe the sun will rise, stand alone and greet the coming night in the last remaining light."

- Chris Cornell

Night has never seemed to scare me as much as the day. Mom or Dad were home sleeping at night. They didn't have somewhere else they had to be—not until my parents divorced and Mom moved away. Still, there were times I woke in the night to listen for my father's snoring. The first night I did not hear it was his first night in the hospital.

Thus, on these new nights of being alone, I had to listen for something else to know that I was not alone. I had to lift my window, even in the winter, to listen and know that I was not alone. Maybe it was the crickets, cicadas, or a muffler hanging by a thread as it scraped against the road when a car drove by. Maybe it was the thunder or the knocking of tree limbs against our home on a stormy evening. Whatever it was, I needed nature when I was alone.

Here I am again, more than forty years later, needing nature more than ever. Those that were there in their reassuring presence, even if they were asleep, are gone—that is, if one is skeptical to protect his or her feelings from the possibility that they might not be here. Night is not as lonely as day for the stars that have been there all my life come out while the thousands of people you could encounter in a day can get by without a word, a smile, or the courtesy of

waiting instead of pushing on by.

Traffic, impatience, and the hope that someone will care all peacefully pass out at night. The sky is clear for the thoughts of a friend and your thoughts to reach one another wherever each of you are in the world—so long as you each are open to and ready for these thoughts to reach one another.

I am nurtured by nature's breeze at this twilight hour. For, I know it carries the thoughts and the spirit of my friend and of me like the thoughts and spirits in us all. These breezes will reach us to remind us that we are not alone and the enthusiasm in our spirit will never die.

I am nurtured by the spirit of my dear friend both in words and nature in itself day and night. With me in the breeze, with me in the twinkle of the stars, and with me in the stillness for it surrounds me with warmth when it is cold and a cool breeze when it is hot. Thank always you for sharing in your spirit.

Nurtured by Nature at Night

"And if you don't believe the sun will rise, stand alone and greet the coming night in the last remaining light."

- Chris Cornell

Night has never seemed to scare me as much as the day. Mom or Dad were home sleeping at night. They didn't have somewhere else they had to be—not until my parents divorced and Mom moved away. Still, there were times I woke in the night to listen for my father's snoring. The first night I did not hear it was his first night in the hospital.

Thus, on these new nights of being alone, I had to listen for something else to know that I was not alone. I had to lift my window, even in the winter, to listen and know that I was not alone. Maybe it was the crickets, cicadas, or a muffler hanging by a thread as it scraped against the road when a car drove by. Maybe it was the thunder or the knocking of tree limbs against our home on a stormy evening. Whatever it was, I needed nature when I was alone.

Here I am again, more than forty years later, needing nature more than ever. Those that were there in their reassuring presence, even if they were asleep, are gone—that is, if one is skeptical to protect his or her feelings from the possibility that they might not be here. Night is not as lonely as day for the stars that have been there all my life come out while the thousands of people you could encounter in a day can get by without a word, a smile, or the courtesy of

waiting instead of pushing on by.

 Traffic, impatience, and
the hope that someone
will care all peacefully
pass out at night. The
sky is clear for the
thoughts of a friend and
your thoughts to reach

one another wherever each of you are in the world—so

long as you each are open to and ready for these

thoughts to reach one another.

I am nurtured by nature's breeze at this twilight

hour. For, I know it carries the thoughts and the spirit

of my friend and of me like the thoughts and spirits in

us all. These breezes will reach us to remind us that we

are not alone and the enthusiasm in our spirit will never

die.

I am nurtured by the spirit of my dear friend both in words and nature in itself day and night. With me in the breeze, with me in the twinkle of the stars, and with me in the stillness for it surrounds me with warmth when it is cold and a cool breeze when it is hot. Thank always you for sharing in your spirit.

Such Glee from Trees

"You know me, I think there ought to be a big old tree right there. And let's give him a friend. Everybody needs a friend."

— Bob Ross

This is one of my favorite streets in the entire world. I don't know anyone that lives on this street. But what I do know is that I have always loved its trees.

They form a living canopy over the street when in full bloom. One not only feels as though they have entered another world when he or she enters this street, but that person feels a sense of peace for sure. For as long as I have known them to stand here, there must be a sense of family and a sense of shared love on this street among the residents for these trees as well as among the trees as well for we know they can love. To love means to protect, to preserve, and to honor.

Many must have worked hard to preserve the lives of these beautiful trees. Thus, when you encounter someone with a mutual love of nature, you have found a kindred spirit of nature.

Oh trees for your memories, I will do my best to honor you gratefully. Oh friend of nature, you have shown me that while nature does not truly belong to us, we still belong in nature.

Nature's Kindred Spirit

"One touch of nature makes the whole world kin."

— William Shakespeare

I think of how some seem to laud themselves for their ancestry. Yes, there may be ancestors to be respected and admired, but wouldn't one of the greatest ways to truly show respect for our ancestors is by honoring them through a similar pattern of hard work to uphold what they were passionate about?

I have come to trust in my belief that the hardest work is done through the constant of showing up. No matter who is there to notice what is done, the person who shows up regardless of who is or is not there truly cares about what he or she is showing up for. His or her consistency demonstrates genuine advocacy.

My dear friend has posed a challenge to me to step out of the house and be a part of nature each day and be accountable for my presence through taking a picture of nature each day. Little would I know how much of a ripple effect this challenge would have on my holistic health, my ability to advocate for beliefs close to my heart through words, and my dreams for the happiness of another person.

Nature! What an unconditionally accepting place to be. The leaves may turn, colors that is, but they don't turn on one another nor anything outside of their species. We may wallow in misery over the waste that has fallen on our heads and shoulders from a bird's behind. But, we know—yes we really do— those heads and shoulders could belong to any of us. They are certainly equal opportunity defecators I'm sure.

There are people that we are reminded of when we are in nature and that remind us of nature when we are in their company. Gentle like a breezy meadow or like a trunk that won't bend or break for the sinister wishes of anyone—yes like the beauty and the loving beast in the giant Redwood tree.

I know a kindred spirit to nature, though I am a little shy to call her out. While she would appreciate the respect and admiration, I can foresee that an excess of either would keep her from what she loves and desires to preserve most—nature itself. Yes, in the breeze I can hear the leaves speak with love for their kindred Chris.

The 13th Spot in Nature
Lake Red Rock

Shadow Webs

"One does not become

enlightened by imagining

figures of light, but by making

the darkness conscious."

-Carl Jung

Whether there is the darkness of space beyond a

blue sky or the authoritarian sun burning bright beyond

the moon, each light leaves a shadow reminding us of

what we must not take for granted.

The connected shadows of a grove of trees

appear to form a web upon the earth. Much like a

spider web captures its prey, this shadow web captures

our attention. Yes, it is fascinating and beautiful, but

all we have to do is imagine the disappearance of any one of these trees to know that we may one day be caught in a falling sky where the last and, therefore, the only shadows we will see will be our own.

The shadows are thus not to be an "oh well," mockery of the efforts of those who are worried about, yet determined and hopeful for, nature. They are, like in the days of pain and struggle of my dear friend Chris, reminders of the determination not to deny, but to overcome these struggles through faith in the greatest muscle in our body and the brightest light in our universe—our heart and soul. I have faith in each of mine because I know that each of hers do and know.

When Nature Finds You

"Rest is not idleness, and to lie sometimes on the grass under trees on a summer's day, listening to the murmur of the water, or watching the clouds float across the sky, is by no means a waste of time."

- Sir John Lubbock

To search is to attempt to control an outcome we may fear. Though, to observe is to trust that the universe will take care of us in our individual destinies. Focusing on a goal with passion is wonderful in reinforcing our confidence and determination. Though, shan't we rest for a moment or two—to surrender to the elements of nature?

Nature can find us in ways that we welcome and ways that we loathe. Thus, how we care for Mother Earth may lend to more forgiving or unforgiving elements of nature.

Today she was still—content like a satiated pride of lions. The breeze blew through her limbs, joints, grasses, manes, and waters with a long and gentle  exhalation. We did not find her sleeping. She found us awake—kindly and gently awake. Therefore, she welcomed this constant of peace emanating from our vulnerable selves.

She knew it was safe to be more than aware, but to seek out. She, nature, warmed the hopeful and cooled the anxious, but was always kind as others walked with her and before her.

It is time for us to whoop our reverence for those among us that have honored our mothers of nature and earth. May we listen to the wisdom in their calm voices and be driven by the enthusiasm in their smiles.

If you are wondering as to who could be such a person among us, look to the northern part of North America. Listen and you will hear the eloquence of Canadian compassion. For, what you hear, what you see, and what you will therefore feel is the warmth to love and the calm to move peacefully through the trials and the joys of life. That is the calm, the compassion, and the peaceful passion of Chris.

**The 15th Spot in Nature
Ewing Park**

The Universe Thanks You for Stopping by

"In three words I can sum up everything I've learned about life: it goes on." – Robert Frost.

Have you ever been a passenger in a vehicle and saw something new on a route you had driven many times before? And, in seeing—well noticing really—what you have discovered, you want to stop and look closer at it right? I hope so at least.

Well, that is the universe for you. It will continue and it will always be there. Nature will continue on its own, probably stronger without us—at least in who we have become. But, it will always give us something new to see and admire.

Nature, like humanity, has a history to be admired. There historians of knowledge. There are also historians of character—those who remember not the facts of history, but feelings throughout history. They remember how a place made them feel or how others felt about events in history that many of us could not imagine the emotions that were connected to them.

We may not remember every tree that once stood where we now stand, but we will remember that there were trees there. We may not see the soil until it is moved to make way for something else. Though, we will remember the rainy days where the soil rose as mud. We will remember how the mud slowed our steps. We will realize the earth below our feet has been here longer than we have. We will realize that no matter how we have covered it whether in gravel, concrete, rubber, or steel, it is our mother's earth, and not our own.

How will we remember all of this if we don't stop to look? How will we remember this if we don't experience it? How will we preserve it if we have not experienced it and, therefore, have an experience to defend?

A friend.

A friend?

Yes, a friend.

A friend that has stopped to see the dangerous fury of others that speed by. She stops to look not with a glance, but an appreciative eye. If you listen to what she says about what she sees, you will see that she is more than seeing it. She is experiencing it. From her footsteps across leaves, twigs, and crunchy grass—

unaltered earth, she is experiencing the connection between the earth and nature above it. From one day being cold to another being a bit warmer, she is experiencing both how we do not control the thermostat for our planet yet our choices leave our planet few options by which it can oblige our likings.

She will come and she will go.

But, she will come back again and again for as long as she can.

And whether in the songs of birds, the breeze through the trees, or the raindrops on the leaves, the universe will find a way to thank her for stopping by.

The 16th Spot in Nature
Thomas Mitchell Park

If You've Seen One
Have You Really Seen Them All?

"In a forest of a hundred

thousand trees, no two

leaves are alike. And no

two journeys along the

same path are alike."

- Paulo Coelho

Many cities and towns have stores in

common. But, each store probably does not

have the same individual people in common as

the other stores. Many parks and other pop-up

spots in nature have similar trees and wildlife in

common, but certainly not the same individual

trees and probably not, depending on migration

patterns, the same individual animals within a

species of wildlife among them.

One bad apple is not like all the other

apples unless you can prove that in tasting them

all. One citizen is not like all others until you

can say that after having met them all. And, by

seeing one tree you certainly have not seen them

all.

Each person is unique with different gifts

and different needs. Each tree in nature is

different with how it benefits the unique needs

of its surroundings in nature and the society of

the land where it stands.

I cannot say what is similar or different

about something in nature or someone in

humanity from afar. I must get out of my home,

get out of my phone, and even get out of my

country and experience each from a truly

palpable distance.

I would never have experienced nature as I

have at this time in my life had it not been for

my friend. And yes, while no friend is like

another, Chris has shown that you can be a

friend to all!

**The 17th Spot in Nature
Downtown Des Moines**

Life Is the Soul of a City
and Nature is the Soul of Life

"It may not feel as if you are in nature when you walk through a city, but you are: All around you is a densely interconnected web of nutrient exchange, competing interests, and cross-species communication. There's an invisible world right in front of our noses, ready for exploration."

—Nathanael Johnson

A part of nature that is cleared for a man-made human need can be devastating to that which lived and thrived in that spot in nature and those that loved that spot in nature and did all they could do for it.

Similarly, a man-made and memories-made piece of society that is vacated for financial, legal, or even personal reasons can be devastating to others. It can break the hearts and the hopes of those that have relied on this place for personal needs and perceived wants that, upon greater examination, are truly understandable needs.

So, when we build or when we vacate, let us do all that we can to honor the memory of what was there to inspire the future care of what and who occupies that location. Let there not be a city block without at least one living piece of nature on that block—whether tree, bush, a garden, or flowers for example.

And let us not forget that not only can we look down or around for nature among us, but we can look up for the nature with wings, nature in a current of wind that brings life to ordinary things, and the nature that falls to bring rise to that which is planted in the earth.

There are souls in a city that laugh, smile, shout, and cry. There are also souls in a city that sway, bob and bounce from flower to flower, and skid along quickly across the pavement after leaping from a branch or limb.

I see the soul of my friend in the acts of kindness and care for the city around me. And I see the soul of my friend in the resolute strength of nature that lives on every block I walk and surrounding many of the buildings I see. This is the gift my friend Chris has given to me.

Seeing One in What One Sees

"What is the good of your stars and trees, your sunrise and the wind, if they do not enter into our daily lives?"

E. M. Forster

Architecture is like gum to me. Its flavor never seems to last.   Nature is an Everlasting Gobstopper of mystical flavor. Though the flavor of nature still lasts longer.

I imagine how I could pull a cloud from the sky as it sticks to my fingers and melts to form a sugary edible sand atop my tongue. I could sip from the lake, like a pool of acai juice, with a straw.

I realize I yearn for the beauty of what once was real to not be restricted to our imagination and the beauty of what is imagined to be real for the betterment of us all. A picture can truly be worth a thousand words, but the direction the camera is pointing tells us which direction the photographer's heart is pointing. And that is how I know in my heart that I can see my good friend Chris in each photo or video she shares even if she herself does not appear in either. I see how she doesn't take a moment for granted in a picture of nature in how she may stop along a path that others may rush beyond. I see her calm in the storms of the world as she finds the beauty of nature that lives beyond our control or power to take it for granted.

In what she sees, says, and the calm of her voice, I am awakened to a stillness in me that sees what is still beautiful about the world and humanity. I was blinded by my grief, but now I can see.

The 19th Spot in Nature

I-80 East Rest Area Near Mitchellville

We Rest with Nature
When We Stop for Nature

If one season can end before another begins, can't we stop at some point in our day to rest? We must give others not only the best of ourselves, but, as we rest, revel in the majesty that none of us is greater than another and no one can do for the world what nature can do. But, there is much we must do for nature so that it can do what it does best!

If we stop and relax, we can see how nature is a little like us. For, a limb on a windy day can joyfully photobomb a picture to say, "Look at me, I am like the ocean waving at you!"

Clouds can be instigators of one's imagination that we are inspired to defend.

"Oh, those may be wispy clouds to you. But, to me those are my guardian angels taking the lead," we might say.

Then, if we imagine the absurd without judgment we can be excited when we see something in a new way—a lesson an adult can learn from a child. For, sometimes the clouds play peak-a-boo with the sun when it pops out like a wide-eyed child at Christmas. And shadows could very well be how the sun paints a picture on the earth.

When we stop for nature, we rest with nature. When we rest with nature we are giving ourselves the opportunity to experience sweet daydreams. Who would stop with you for nature? Who would rest with you and nature too? I can think of a friend from far away that would rest with me, even if resting far away, and would call out pictures in the clouds or call out a bird, a limb, or an errant leaf for sneaking into our view.

Yes, that is the joy of what my friend Chris would do!

The 20th Spot in Nature
Ewing Park
and the Ashley Oakland Star Park

We Are All Pioneers
of Our Own Imaginations

"People who end up as 'first' don't actually set out to be first. They set out to do something they love."

- Condoleezza Rice

"The person who follows the crowd will usually go no further than the crowd. The person who walks alone is likely to find himself in places no one has ever seen before."

- Albert Einstein

It is not just another day. It is not just another park. And it is certainly not just another tree.

"It's you Oakie!" I can just imagine one tree saying to another in building up that other.

"Nah, it's all you Oaks!" I bet he would humbly reply.

Then, in looking up at their limbs and branches then down upon the glimmering grass, it is as though they have made shadow animals on the ground.

As I walk alongside the muddy creek, I can see my reflection in the shallow water and imagine the fairytale magic mirror itself.

"Mirror mirror in the creek. Who's your favorite passerby this week?" I think to myself with a chuckle.

And, in the light of day I can imagine how the trees would, if they could, come to life in a loose and limber way at night. For, then the sun will set like the

of your parents' car as it drives off and you open the

doors to your first school dance. And the moon will

hover over the earth like a disco ball over the dance

floor.

With its strong and captivating limbs raised like a

dance floor paramour, you can just hear that tree shout

in freeing glee with the music, "Raise your limbs like

you just don't care. Feel the rush of the midnight air."

One might ask how I could have risked such a

foolish frenzy of words to describe nature like this.

Well, it couldn't have been realized without a

spotter like Chris that catches you when you try to run

and keeps you from holding back. A pioneer without

fear!

Grounding Ourselves in What We All Have in Common

"The Earth is what we all have in common."
-Wendell Berry

 Each day our beliefs, feelings, and our experiences will certainly be different—to at least some degree. Our passion for these beliefs, feelings, and experiences may create distance from or conflict with other people. It may be hard for us to find something we agree upon as motivation for a resolution to this conflict. The known statement, "We must agree to disagree," will certainly come to mind so that we may at least be able go our separate ways.

Though, what, especially in these uncertain times, if we discovered that what we have in common could be in danger. It could be the shared space of a business that operated in our community for our entire lives that is now hit hard by weak economic times. It could even a natural disaster that could threaten the closure of this shared space. Resources like water are threatened by droughts and pollution. And the earth itself that we stand on is threatened by eminent domains, contamination, and erosion.

Without a healthy and safe environment humanity is certainly threatened—even if we don't always acknowledge that we have done it to ourselves. Without a care for this environment, we have given up on thriving—even surviving—altogether. And without a love for our environment, we have given up on the joys of today and tomorrow.

My friend Chris, at thousands of miles away, shares, and far exceeds quite honestly, the same sun, the same stars in the sky, the same air, and the same love and never-ending hopes for a beautiful nature on our planet as I do. Yes, I have talked about it far more than I have walked that walk. Though I know that her footsteps, her breaths of fresh nature air, and her care towards every creature along her path is her walking the walk of a talk like mine.

Let the ground itself be a peaceful and beautiful place for us to walk with nature. Let us make the earth itself the common ground that nature and humanity share. Chris can. We can. She does. And so too will we!

A Promise to Keep

"The woods are lovely dark and deep, but I have promises to keep…" —Robert Frost

Oh daylight! The joy and possibilities that we

hope it brings. Sure, it can and often does bring what we hope. Consider, though, how we can be seen and we can be avoided in the day. Someone can know specifically who we are and walk the other way. Don't we do that with nature as well? We can admire a place in nature and go on our way. We can scoff at the litter, the vandalism, and the neglect in that very same place one year later and…still go on our way. Our admiration was practically a promise just like a child begging for a puppy and telling mom or dad that that he or she would feed it, give it water, take it outside every day, and always love it just so he or she could have it. Then, the child loses interest or sees that this responsibility is too much and abandons care of this sweet animal to where Mom and Dad hopefully step in for the sake of the animal.

We ask for a park and we say how much we love a park. But, do we care for that park? Where is our promise?

What if the woods are our promise? What if the dark and deep in us is what is most lovely? One can't see me to know that I am not the tall and maybe not the handsome of the tall, dark, and handsome. But, those are relative to nature and humanity right?

Yes, the woods are my promise. The woods are nature and nature is the woods. I made a promise to myself to more than just take a picture of nature in the miles I must go before my sleep. I made a promise to express the deep appreciation I have acquired for nature as a result of my friend Chris' encouragement that got me out the door and out of my head to where nature could enter my soul. I made the promise to myself to express my appreciation in these words in this book—for Chris!

Nature Can Be a Beast—a Beautiful Beast

"You can't argue with a river – it is going to flow. You can dam it up, put it to useful purposes, you can deflect it, but you can't argue with it."

– Dean Acheson

Is it possible that we use words like "beast," and "beauty," in mutual comparisons to exhibit control? Maybe to suppress our authentic thoughts and feelings—truths we try to deny? Yes, like the pairing of judgments of character and judgments of appearance. Might such vile and shaming pairings of words be like a dam trying to hold back the waters we fear?

No, the dam is not nature. The water is. The damn cannot keep the water from doing what it has set out to do—flow. For, it may be stopped momentarily.

But, it will swirl then it will rise. Imagine the high

wave of water behind a dam like a professional wrestler

jumping off of the top turnbuckle of a ring and landing

with a giant frog splash on his opponent.

That is the recognized fury of the water. The beautiful beast it is. Even a beast that fights back if provoked. A beast determined to move.

My dear friend is a beauty in the trifecta of the human condition.   Just like beautiful

calm waters. Though, when the odds and symptoms

taunt her, she is a beast of determination—a beautiful

beast of course.

A Rainy Day Is Nature's Sunday

"Rain is grace; rain is the sky descending to the earth; without rain, there would be no life."

- John Updike

A rainy day is a day for nature to rest and be rehydrated by the sky. The wet and grey day cools and softens the fractured earth. It sends the fair-weather folk fleeing for the calmer and warmer climates for the novices of nature.

One might call it a pool break or a coffee break for nature. Mother Earth can soak in the showers and work out her kinks from the many steps that have been

taken upon her. The sky can breathe as the smog

dissipates.

 And I, on nature's Sunday,

can tend to this literary

garden of syntax and

semantics in the verbal

vegetation I am growing for

my dear friend.

This is your blossoming bouquet, your harvest, and

your field forever my dear friend. This is the nature I

have tried to capture and the harvest of gratitude I have

grown for you.

Get a Little Closer Now
...to Nature and Each Other

"...whatever happens to the world, the river never stops responding to the friendly breeze with its murmuring sound of joyfulness."

—Munia Khan, Attainable

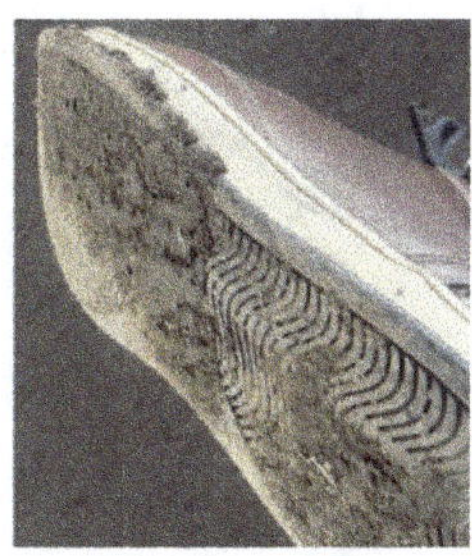

"Sometimes it takes a little mud on your shoe to get a better view."

—Michael Irving

From all of those in someone's life that have passed away or those have decided to leave someone's life where they were like family or a friend to that someone, meeting others again for the first time can be a traumatic effort in itself. In using myself as an

 example, I wearily wonder

who will stay and who will

leave without, as they have

historically done, a farewell

or an explanation.

Though, when anyone leaves,

there is always something left behind.

Think of a tree that has shed all of its leaves or

whose blossoms have wilted from the cold and have

blown away. There still stands a trunk with limber

limbs conducted by the wind.

Memories have settled into our minds with

feelings as bright as a new pair of suede shoes or as

blue as a pair of jeans that have fought off fading. The

tree will grow and grow—some days slowly it seems.

It doesn't take our company for granted in the shade it

provides and it is never without reassurance in being there for us to lean on when we think we are otherwise alone. Then, one day like that where you see family that you haven't seen since the last holiday that brought you together, you will find that it has grown to unimaginable heights in its trunk and depths in its roots like a child growing in height or voice and deeper in voice and wisdom.

That tree may stand alone. Though, it still can grow closer to other trees. Its blossoms touch other blossoms and we are drawn to nature's artistry in their development.

If two leaves, and certainly more, can grow together on the same branch for the life of a tree, can we grow up together and live together in the same humanity?

I believe for those that have shared a space, as a

stranger sitting nearby on a bench or a loved one at the

same table, we can both

definitely see what Chris can

do, what we can do, in what

two leaves can do for a tree, for

you, and for humanity!

Our Vows with Nature

"To pass through this brief life as nature demands. To give it up without complaint. Like an olive that ripens and falls. Praising its mother, thanking the tree it grew on."

—Marcus Aurelius

In looking through two trees, I believe I have found the life— definitely the spirit—that they inherited. Nature does not allow us to be condemned to the ground, but to rise from it and inspire peace and nurturing with those who roam amongst it. Mother Earth has welcomed our residency and Mother Nature has done all she can to nurture us with the company she has raised in all of the living things that surround us.

That is one of many vows Mother Earth and Mother Nature have made to us. Though, what are our vows to Mother Earth and Mother Nature? Have we forgotten them? Do we even know what they are?

What would nature hope our vows to be? Might they be something like…

We will leave this land as you have left it for us.

We will share the stories of the joy we have shared with you with our children to inspire their love for you as well.

We will honor that you came before us to ensure that you are there for those that come after us.

Today I am with nature. Tomorrow I may be a part of nature myself. Let us do all we can to make tomorrow possible for all of us--especially the nature that we love—the nature that includes us.

My Neighborhood at Night

The Nature of the Night
Is a Special Nature to Me

 "Just 'cause you can't see it, doesn't mean it, isn't there."

—Brad Delson, Chester Charles Bennington, Dave Farrell, Francis White, Joseph Hahn, Mike Shinoda, Robert G. Bourdon —Linkin Park. "One More Light."

I have heard that if we lose one of our five senses, like sight or hearing for example, that our remaining senses become stronger. So, though there may not be as much that we think we can see of nature at night, this may afford us the opportunity to listen to what the hustle and bustle of society clouds of nature for us during the day.

You may be able to hear the pine needle branches combing through the evening breeze or oak leaves fanning the wind. They may be too dark to see, but what you hear of their shuffling in the breeze and their waltzes with the wind both will let you know that they are there and strong in their presence.

Though clouds most often make their auditory presence known when they are active in a storm of some kind, there are precious opportunities to see them at the night. They appear like that glow below a child's blanket when he or she stays up past bedtime hours to read a book that can't be put down under the glow of a flashlight "borrowed" from

Mom and Dad.

The nature of the night is neither to be taken for

granted in its beauty nor in what it does for the earth.

The beautiful creatures and foliage of the night are the

night watchmen that make nature possible for the next

day.

At a Meadow's End, Nature's Secret Begins

"Those who contemplate the beauty of the earth find reserves of strength that will endure as long as life lasts."

—Rachel Carson

Thinking of nature and speaking to it from my dark bedroom late on a lonely night does not always bring the variety of life within it closer. Though, like the many times I walked in nature along paths formed by human feet-- deeper into the woods like those I have explored with my daughter, I find that I have reached a special place where I am with what lives in nature and those that live on in my heart and soul.

It is untouched—beautiful in how no man, woman, or child could have made it this way. Yes, it is natural beauty like that of each of us when we awake and start our day. Yes, we are beautiful each day from the moment we open our eyes through every moment we are asleep.

How dare I make a mockery of the bedhead  disheveled? But, no I do not. For, I believe, in our fatigued vulnerability, we are most beautiful then as we are natural, untouched, and authentic without a care as to the judgments of others. This is the hidden beauty of nature that is untouched. It is welcoming in its authenticity and vulnerability.

Nature does not blush nor cower from our judgments. As it does not try to impress us, we are naturally in awe of its fury and beauty. We can sit with it as it is and it will be with us as we are without a word in the peace and acceptance of one another's company.

There I was at the end of my rope where each strand was once a loved one now lost and the last strand was now me. Chris revealed how nature would be there to catch me and comfort me in its unconditional acceptance of my presence. I could be vulnerable. Yes, I could be the hidden, but true, me.

A friend of nature like Chris will show you her or his vulnerable self and welcome yours too. There is not anyone else you have to be in nature. Just you. Nature will be there for you. Chris will too.

The Lapping of Luxury

"Wilderness is not a luxury, but a necessity of the human spirit."

— Edward Abbey.

Luxury, itself, suggests a frivolous exploitation of our resources. But, what if the luxury of nature itself is a frivolous exploitation of our time and resources that could have been spent elsewhere other than in nature itself?

Should we not waste our time doing something other than sitting at home? Should we not waste the opportunity to pour out our resources on material luxuries that will go out of style?

We can certainly choose and our choices themselves will not justify judgments against us. But, nature will still be there—hopefully, so long as we don't leave the excess of our luxuries behind thinking she will know how to handle them.

So, which is a necessity to you—something that brings you beauty today or the beauty that you share every day in the surroundings and company of all that is alive and with you in spirit?

The waters will roll and lap against the shore. But, they will return—not once, but many times more. May you

honor the luxury of peace and comfort that our nature and earth mothers offer you—unconditionally to the point that you care for them too.

They love you too. I didn't realize the unconditional acceptance and love that Mother Nature and Mother Earth shared with us until I saw how they came to life in the nature Chris encouraged me to step out of my isolation and see. Yes, from the skies I see to the seas I see.

How Awesome to Blossom

"Water your dreams with fear, and they will wilt; with doubt, and they will wither; with hope, and they will grow; with faith, and they will flourish."

—Matshona Dhliwayo

How inspiring is the determination of a bud to

blossom by its own volition. It relies on faith in there being sunny days and days of rain. The blossom may not think of what winter can do. Does it know? Does it matter whether or not it does?

As my hopeful self believes, there is a soul in that blossom's tree dashing from its roots to its trunk to its limbs to its branches to where the bud will grow again.

Nature reminds us not just of life and death, but of the rising like a phoenix from the roots again and again in another beautiful creation of nature and humanity. That bud, I believe, was once an elder—a seasoned veteran of the wilderness—that has returned to learn something new and apply the gifts of its soul to the betterment of all life seen and unseen surrounding it.

My dear friend's health and well-being may be the elephant in the room we are afraid to talk about for fears of dwelling on a sad truth. But, she knows and she has been determined to engrave her legacy of love

and optimism on every brick in the road of her journey.

Her walk is silent only for moments to listen to nature

then it is melodic from her words of appreciation for it

and her belief in others she meets on her path.

Her legacy will blossom in our appreciation for

nature, for others, and for the moments of life

themselves. Is it not awesome how a heart and soul,

like that of a tree, can blossom!

Closer Views Bring Buddings Anew

"Nature does not hurry, yet everything is accomplished."

— Lao Tzu

Nature, for good reasons, does not accommodate the impatient, the aggressive, or the hard to please. It

doesn't take orders or special requests and, though it offers much that is pleasing to the senses, it is not a people-pleasing entity in all of the life it encompasses.

For the patient, the curious, and the gentle, nature inspires a love, wonder, and excitement in all of its minute happenings like that between a newborn baby and his or her family. Nature and that little miss or fella both capture our eyes and theirs follow us like the moon and the stars that seemingly follow you at night. For, you are not just that little baby's world in how he or she depends on you. You are also nature's world too.

You are the neighbors the birds wish to live with. They are nature's alarm clock and yours too with more inviting melodies when you wake up than the average alarm clock I'm sure. You are like a proud parent to the trees around you in how you share your pride about being there when each tree was planted to being there still to see their enormous growth.

Your day is busy, I know. But, what would you do if, for a moment, you let all that makes you busy just go? It will still be there. But, what if you took that moment and stopped to look closer at one tree that you passed daily? You don't even have to imagine what you would see or smell of its buds and blossoms. You don't have to imagine because seeing it up close and taking in its sweet smell is more than you can imagine.

That is what we realize in the time we stop to say more than what we fill obligated to say to another person. It is what we realize when we listen and take notice of how we feel in that interaction. And, as I truly believe, our feelings make our memories stronger—eternal.

I would not have made the dear friendship I have with Chris had it not been for the walk she encouraged me to take with nature. I would not have something to look forward to or write about the next day had it not been for this challenge we shared in taking one picture in nature each day.

All that I have written here is not just for Chris and those who I know will be inspired by the sincerity of her curiosity, compassion, wit, and wisdom. This is for everyone to honor Chris in their lives or to meet her in these words if they have not had a chance to meet her before, very sadly, she is gone. What has taken over her life will one day take her life. But, nothing will take away her spirit, her dreams, and what we have come to know and love about her—her eternal legacy.

This is also for my daughter for her and the world to know that we don't grow alone. Like the limb from which the leaves grow until they are on their own and where that tree will never leave but always be there for that leaf I will be that tree too--always there for you. I love your will to wonder and wander.

It is Chris L'Amarca's nature to nurture. May we nurture her legacy as we remember her in the gentle strength and beauty of the nature she loves and we love too. That is what makes her and nature both…

L'Amarcable!

Epilogue: No Time for Whenever

Habits of success are great, so long as you don't have an overabundance of need for recognition from others for what you have achieved. Habits of service open doors to others being there for you in your time of need. Success is communicated through telling. Service is communicated through doing.

Chris has been one that does more than she tells. For, the more that she tells of what she does, the less time she has to do what she wants to for you. It is not done just in making the best of a shorter life. It is done to open doors for me and for you.

On a day that it is harder for her to walk in nature, she still does her best to be among it. She rides her bike in nature. She walks or rides as far as she can then she sits with nature. She knows she doesn't have time to think of what she cannot do. In fact, I believe she rarely asks for another's help in doing much of anything. She will not wait for them to respond and she knows that if they can't make up their minds then they never truly wanted to be there anyway.

She is the "I can't wait," while many of us are the "Maybe later." She is the one counting the ripples from the raindrops falling on a lake while the rest are the ones waiting for the rain to stop and the sun to come out—whenever that may be.

Chris lives many miles from me and, believe it or not, I have not yet met her in person. I therefore thank both technology and nature for being matchmakers for a great friendship.

As I write this at 11:43 p.m. on April 19, 2023, a storm has just caused me to lift my head from its flash of light through my window. It clapped its last clap of thunder and it cried its last drop of rain. Storms come and go though we don't have time to wait for whenever each may be. We find beauty in their absence and know that they cannot touch what is most beautiful of all in their presence. Though there will be inevitable sadness when Chris is not here, there will be the peace, compassion, and beauty of nature—the nature of her spirit in nature—that she will always be a part of which will always be a part of us. And no, we have no time to wonder whenever that may be. All you have to do is just be with nature, be with those you care about, or be with a stranger or two. All you have to do to know she is there is not to try, but to just "be."

Appendix:

Captured in Canada by Chris

These are some of the many pictures that Chris has taken and shared with me on her daily walks and bicycle rides in the nature of Canada. Her daily journeys in nature inspired me in her determination to be out in nature, her soothing voice in the narrated videos she would also send, and her positive focus on the beauty of nature itself. I am honored to share what she has shared with me.

There was a day that Chris was feeling under the weather and, as I am sure nature would agree, needed to rest. Though, in her devotion to nature, she captured the nature that keeps her company and that she cares for at home.